DESIGNER SCRAPBOOKS with

Brenda Walton

DESIGNER SCRAPBOOKS with

Brenda Walton

Sterling Publishing Co., Inc.
New York
A Sterling/Chapelle Book

Chapelle, Ltd.
P.O. Box 9252, Ogden, UT 84409
(801) 621-2777 • (801) 621-2788 Fax
e-mail: chapelle@chapelleltd.com
Web site: www.chapelleltd.com

Library of Congress Cataloging-in-Publication Data

Walton, Brenda.
  Designer scrapbooks with Brenda Walton.
    p. cm.
  "A Sterling/Chapelle Book."
  Includes index.
  ISBN 1-4027-2197-8
1. Photographs--Conservation and restoration. 2. Photograph
albums. 3. Scrapbooks. I. Title.

TR465.W35 2006
745.593--dc22
                                2005025305
10 9 8 7 6 5 4 3 2 1

Published by Sterling Publishing Co., Inc.
387 Park Avenue South, New York, NY 10016
©2006 by Brenda Walton
Distributed in Canada by Sterling Publishing
c/o Canadian Manda Group, 165 Dufferin Street
Toronto, Ontario, Canada M6K 3H6
Distributed in the United Kingdom by GMC Distribution Services,
Castle Place, 166 High Street, Lewes, East Sussex, England BN7 1XU
Distributed in Australia by Capricorn Link (Australia) Pty. Ltd.
P. O. Box 704, Windsor, NSW 2756, Australia
Printed and Bound in China
All Rights Reserved

Sterling ISBN 1-4027-2197-8

For information about custom editions,
special sales, premium and corporate purchases,
please contact Sterling Special Sales Department
at 800-805-5489 or specialsales@sterlingpub.
com.

Every effort has been made to ensure that all information in this book is accurate. However, due to differing conditions, tools, and individual skills, the publisher cannot be responsible for any injuries, losses, and/or other damages, which may result from the use of the information in this book.

This volume is meant to stimulate crafting ideas. If readers are unfamiliar or not proficient in a skill necessary to attempt a project, we urge that they refer to an instructional book specifically addressing the required technique.

Dedication

For my parents, Bill and Gloria,
who taught me the pure joy of creating;
and for Doug and Aaron, who inspired me
to share that joy with others.

Contents

The Beginning

Discovering Inspiration in Everyday Life

My life as an artist evolved from a childhood filled with love, joyous laughter, music, and varied creative crafting projects. From the time I was a young child, I have always enjoyed painting, drawing, and crafting. Throughout my academic career, I was constantly encouraged to pursue my passion for art by my parents, friends, and a series of talented and supportive teachers. While an art major at California State University, Sacramento, I studied jewelry making, ceramics, and printmaking, while focusing on painting and drawing. I eventually earned a master's degree in art in 1977. At the time, I had no idea what I might do with my new degree. I only had a distant dream of someday working as a professional artist.

Travel has always been an important part of my life. Shortly after college, I set out on an adventure that would significantly influence the direction of my interests. For two years, I

worked and traveled throughout New Zealand, my mother's homeland. I learned to truly appreciate the beauty of nature and the awe-inspiring environment that surrounded me. The exotic tropical flowers and fruits were a great source of delight and became the subject of my drawings and paintings. It was a wonderful time of exploration and discovery. I experimented with new forms of artistic expression, which confirmed my belief that

art would always be part of my life.

While traveling in New Zealand, I discovered my love of calligraphy. It all began with a gift from a dear friend—a two-dollar instructional book on hand-lettering, a broad-edged pen, and a bottle of ink. I quickly became intrigued by the art of calligraphy and began filling my journals with decorative words and images.

Upon my return to California, I began taking classes and seriously studying calligraphy. My interest in lettering took me to London, New York, Portland, Rome, and San Francisco in order to further my experience and to study with several world-renowned calligraphers. In 1979, my husband, Doug, and I launched a small calligraphy business specializing in hand-lettered wedding invitations. That work eventually led to commissions for book jackets, logotypes, and greeting cards. It still amazes me that an entire career could be built on such a simple beginning.

The birth of our son, Aaron, in 1981 coincided with the realization that my dream of becoming a full-time professional artist could come true. Doug's innate business sense and foresight gave me the support and courage to make that dream a reality. In between caring for our young son and teaching calligraphy classes, Doug and I developed a plan to expand our business by working with graphic design firms and advertising agencies on a broader scale. Thanks to some good

luck and a lot of hard work, I have been happily occupied with a continuous stream of challenging and diverse projects ever since. We are now proudly affiliated with a select group of highly respected licensees who are responsible for the manufacture and distribution of quality products featuring my designs for scrapbooking, wall coverings, china, fabric, stationery, and crafts products, many of which are now available worldwide.

In 1998, I began what has developed into an extremely creative licensing relationship with K&Company. Together with Kay Stanley, an amazingly talented designer and businesswoman, we have developed more than a dozen innovative and popular scrapbooking collections. Beginning with a line of albums, embossed stickers, and coordinating papers, our collections have now expanded to include metal and fabric tags, rub-on transfers, clear domes, and ornate metal charms.

Responding to customer interest in handmade cards, we developed "Beyond Postmarks," a complete card-making program of patterned die-cut cards, decorative papers, embellishments, and a companion project book, *Brenda Walton's Handmade Cards*. Each new collection

brings with it opportunities to expand my creative horizons and to experiment with new styles and techniques. I'm proud of the work that has been produced with K&Company. The high level of quality and the diversity of the product line is unparalleled in the craft industry.

Travel continues to be one of the greatest influences on my work. On our many travels, Doug and I enjoy visiting art museums, antique fairs, and flea markets; going for long walks; chatting with the local residents; and shopping (research!). Everywhere I look, something sparks my imagination. I am a collector of all things vintage, and I love to find ways to incorporate ephemera and everyday materials into my papercrafting projects. You will find old buttons, watch faces, postcards, vintage trims, and ribbons sprinkled throughout the layouts and cards featured in this book. I think they add a great deal of personality and charm to projects and immediately imbue them with a sense of history.

I consider myself extremely fortunate to be making a living as a painter and designer. I look forward to coming into my studio each morning and starting to "work." I have the good fortune of being surrounded with a very capable and talented team of creative professionals. The air is full of possibilities! Every day is another opportunity to be inspired, explore new ideas and develop new product concepts. I am very grateful to all those who support my work and make it possible to continue doing what I love.

Wishing you a lifetime of inspiration,

I am beginning to learn that it is the sweet, simple things in life that are the real ones, after all.

Laura Ingalls Wilder

Introduction

Scrapbooking is a delightful way to preserve the priceless memories of a beautiful wedding or a surprise birthday celebration. It's also a loving documentation of the simple pleasures found in everyday life, whose significance may be not be revealed until years later. These moments that fill a scrapbook can be as small and seemingly insignificant as a day at the beach building sandcastles, a meaningful hug between a father and son, or a grandmother baking her legendary cookies. These sweet memories and simple delights reflect the essence of who we really are.

Although photos and mementos are the main focus of many scrapbooks, I also enjoy the personal expression found in the text featured in the layouts. Scrapbooking invites crafters to capture memories with meaningful headlines, witty expressions, and poignant reflections. Scrapbooking is a valuable creative outlet and has become an important way

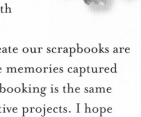

to honor lives, commemorate experiences, and share memories with generations to come, both through images and words.

The steps we take to create our scrapbooks are as personal and unique as the memories captured inside. My approach to scrapbooking is the same as my approach to other creative projects. I hope these three guidelines will help you become more expressive with your own scrapbooking.

Surround yourself with sources of inspiration.

I am a collector of all things quirky, interesting, and colorful. Whether it's a Victorian brooch, a length of richly patterned ribbon, or a swatch of vintage fabric, I bring it into my home to keep and display. I find that even though an item may not relate to a current project, it may one day inspire me in some unexpected way.

My studio is filled with jars of colored buttons, stacks of books, drawers filled with patterned papers, and boxes of ribbons. I have a large inspiration board near my drawing table that is covered with swatches of beautiful fabric, paper flowers, and letters from dear friends. Everywhere I look, I see something beautiful that inspires me. You can encourage your own creativity by surrounding yourself with fun and inspirational objects that you can easily acquire at antique fairs, flea markets, and secondhand shops.

I also recommend keeping a journal to record anything remarkable that delights you or catches your eye. I keep a small sketch book in my purse and fill it with thumbnail drawings, miniature photos, and notes about all the extraordinary things that excite me, whether walking through a neighborhood in my hometown or exploring a London flower market. My journals serve as handy references back at the studio and become the basis for many future projects.

Discover your own personal style.

I enjoy teaching scrapbooking workshops because it gives me a chance to see the many creative ways crafters use the products I've designed. I am constantly amazed by the tremendous range of expression. The diversity shown in the scrapbook layouts is a reflection of the crafter's own personal style. I encourage you to mix colors and patterns, create interesting textures and layers, and to add dimension with vintage accents. By experimenting with new techniques and materials you will discover your own unique and beautiful style.

Share your creations with family and friends.

For me, crafting with family and friends of all ages is a great source of inspiration, and noticeably recharges my creativity. I enjoy working in an environment in which I can see the use of new materials and innovative techniques. Let others see your work, and ask to see theirs.

I regularly craft with a group of five talented artists who live in different parts of the country. We meet once a year, each bringing a creative crafting project and all the materials needed. We spend several days sharing valuable tips and techniques on crafting, music, cooking, and relationships. The most marvelous and unexpected creations come out of these fun get-togethers.

Whether you are new to scrapbooking or an experienced crafter, I hope this book inspires you to explore unfamiliar techniques or combine unexpected colors and patterns. Try something new and experience the joy that comes from innovation!

Do ordinary things with extraordinary love.
Mother Theresa

And the secret garden bloomed and bloomed,
and every day revealed new secrets.
Frances Hodgson Burnett

A Word from Brenda

Designer Scrapbooks with Brenda Walton is a showcase of my favorite scrapbooking layouts created over the last two years. The projects are arranged by technique so you can use these examples both as an inspirational tool and an instructional crafting guide. The crafting styles I describe range from simple to challenging but they're all fun. You'll be surprised how these simple ideas can bring your pages to a whole new level. In addition to my favorite layouts, I have also included some paper-crafting examples, so when you finish your scrapbook you can delight your friends with a handmade card or tag created with leftover papers and embellishments.

Scrapbooking provides virtually unlimited opportunities to be creative and express yourself. The examples presented in this book will inspire you to create finished and professional-quality layouts. Bring a sense of history to your layouts by incorporating vintage elements. See how translucent materials like vellum and sheer fabric can instantly add depth and interest to your layouts. Create your own original paper backgrounds using stamps and stencils. Explore the expressive use of words and letters using die-cut stickers, or create your own headlines and text using a personal computer. You will enjoy discovering how you can transform your papers and photos in innovative and interesting ways.

For my
dear friend
(Patricia)

EXTRA QUALITY

PEARL ONIONS

chapter **1**

Mixing it Up

Combining Colors & Patterns

Bring a refreshing twist to layouts with unexpected colors and patterns.

Party Doll Vintage paper-doll dress cutouts are a delightful way to introduce new colors and patterns. Collect Victorian ephemera and let the unique vintage shapes inspire expressive layouts.

Sisters Geometric and floral patterns combine with an assortment of coordinating embellishments to create a refreshing background for cherished photos.

Aaron at 24 By placing decorative papers from the same color family in a geometric grid design, a surprisingly wide variety of patterns can harmonize successfully on one page.

Floral Birthday Card & Birthday Boy Tag
Make a special embellishment into a sensational focal point by showcasing it against a complementary paper pattern as was done for this card and tag.

birthday
boy

super star

time wit

BIRTHDAY
Fun

Mr. and Mrs. Stephen Herrin
October 8, 1995

Mr. and Mrs. S. William Meehan
request the honor of your presence
at the marriage of their daughter
Sheila Jane
to
Mr. Stephen Herrin
Sunday, October the eighth
nineteen hundred and ninety-five
at three o'clock in the afternoon

Chanticleer
Mountain Road
California

Garden Wedding I Create an impressive two-page layout and expand the visual space by bridging the center seam with one common sheet of decorative paper.

And the secret garden
bloomed and bloomed
and every day revealed
new miracles

LOVE

HEART
to heart

Garden Wedding II Dimensional blossoms, cut from the background floral paper and
adhered with foam dots, add another level of coordinating pattern and color.

Pink Gift Bag & Orange Gift Bag
A combination of complementary patterns
and trims enhances this set of miniature
gift bags.

NANCY, ELINOR
AND ELIZABETH
June 1935

Elinor & Sisters Springtime florals and a variety of geometric patterns encircle
the featured heritage photo and create a vibrant and refreshing page design.

One sunny Sunday, we were headed down the highway to pick fresh strawberries. Suddenly, we came upon an entire field of colorful delphinium! We quickly hopped out of the car and ran over to get a closer look at the spectacular pink, purple and white stalks, almost as tall as the girls!

happiness

sweet memories

Cousins Elaborately decorated alphabet stickers become a patterned element that adds texture and variety to whimsical layouts.

Happiness Patterned tags and frames become bright complements to a lively
layout sprinkled with coordinating stickers, ribbons, and embellishments.

a lovelier

flower on earth

was never sown.

e

i

n

g

best friends

GIRL

chapter **2**

From the Heart

Designing Expressive Layouts with Text

*Discover how words can become an important
and beautiful design element.*

WHERE are you going

my little one, little one?

Where are you going

my baby, my own?

Turn around

and you're two

Turn around

and you're four

Turn around

and you're a young one

Going out of the door.

emma elizabeth
robin and jim's wedding
june 2001

Emma Elizabeth Short lines from a sentimental poem create an interesting graphic collage element when cut into strips and arranged playfully down the page.

the wOrld

is sO full

Of a number

of things

I'm sure

we shOuld all

be as happy

as Kings.

robert louis stevenson

SUMMER TIME climbing THE

fiShing kAleidOscopes

CIRCUS

snAkes & sNailS

peAnut buTteR frOgs

to the moon

time with sand castles

DAD wORMS

snAkes & sNailS

Peanut buTteR frOgs
and Jelly

lukey, orion
and aaron

summer 1988

endless
summer

DREAMS

Dreams Use papers filled with words and expressions to quickly create fun and unique photo frames.
Add another level of interest by layering, grommeting, and sanding gently with extra-fine sandpaper.

Paris, 1925 A variety of font styles complements the playful and
eclectic nature of this charming heritage layout.

Nested Boxes
Create a unique set of
storage boxes for treasured
photos and ephemera.
Embellish the exteriors with
heritage expressions and
decorate the interiors with
copies of family letters for a
personal touch.

Sweet Mother Card
(Left) By using a combination of paper stickers and clear dome letters, a decorative tag becomes the focal point of this heartfelt card.

Vintage Tea Party Card
(Below) A dimensional word frame instantly adds whimsy and charm to a sweet heritage photo.

All Girl Combine word embellishments, such as stickers, tags, and transfers, to playfully describe someone special without the need for handwritten journaling.

Love You Darling I A series of heartfelt telegrams pieced together creates an unexpected border design.

Love You Darling II The lyrics to a treasured love song evoke sweet memories of a wartime romance that has endured for more than 60 years.

Together Big Sister little brother

Lauren and Ian have always been so close. They do everything together and Lauren is very protective of her sweet little brother.

LAUREN

IAN

Together Word transfers layered over patterned papers create a feeling of subtle sophistication.

Love's Trinity

Soul, heart, and body, we thus singly name,
Are not in love divisible and distinct,
But each with each inseparably link'd.
One is not honour, and the other shame,
But burn as closely fused as fuel, heat, and flame.

They do not love who give the body and keep
The heart ungiven; nor they who yield the soul,
And guard the body. Love doth give the whole;
Its range being high as heaven, as ocean deep,
Wide as the realms of air or planet's curving sweep.

—ALFRED AUSTIN

MY HEART'S DESIRE

Forever Oversized, contemporary alphabet stickers bring a fresh
and modern touch to elegant wedding photos.

a lovelier

flower on earth

was never sown.

shakespeare

forever IN MY *heart*

Forever in My Heart Print a favorite classic quote from your home
computer to make layouts truly personal and unique.

Kate Box
Create a personalized keepsake box for a friend
and showcase her name with playful, oversized
alphabet stickers.

chapter **3**

On the Surface

Building Interest with Textures & Embellishments

Layer a variety of three-dimensional elements
to create impressive depth and detail.

Sweet Friend Metal charms and embellishments add textural variety
when combined with decorative papers and ribbon.

dear HEART

SWEET Friend

THANK YOU

Gift Tags
Ordinary tags become fresh and
interesting page embellishments
when decorated with assorted
three-dimensional stickers and
colorful ribbons.

darling SISTER

r OBIN

Hold a true
FRIEND
with both your
hands.

sweet

lOve

of friendship

Vintage Classroom An elegant length of richly colored ribbon is attached
with a classic wax seal to evoke the spirit of a bygone era.

Hope & Devotion Add dimension to existing patterned papers by cutting out selected shapes
and elevating them with foam dots. Coordinating buttons add a distinctive touch.

Sierra A playful headline is created from a series of dimensional patterned tags suspended from a colorful ribbon.

June 2004

LOVE

Julia Card & Amy Card
Dimensional alphabet stickers add another layer of interest
and a personal touch to handmade cards.

Dress Card & Niece Card
Use existing or handmade three-dimensional embellishments
to create the focal point for a special invitation or card.

Party Favor Bag
A simple party favor bag is made even more
adorable when decorated with dimensional
stickers and colorful grosgrain ribbon.

By the Sea Coordinate the patterns and colors of dimensional
embellishments to help unify a themed layout.

Purse Gift Tags
Layer clear domed stickers on top of velvet
or grosgrain ribbons to create charming gift
cards, place cards, and tags.

Believe An exuberant combination of three-dimensional
embellishments adds height, texture, and interest.

chapter 4

Vintage Charm

Enhancing Layouts with Collected Treasures

*Add warmth and personality by incorporating
your favorite collectibles and ephemera.*

Tea Party A vintage family photograph makes a charming
cover for this mini photo album.

Sewing Box
The classic embellishments adorning this oval
gift box hint at its intended use.

Sweet Baby Give a contemporary photo timeless elegance by adding
vintage metal embellishments and coordinating ribbons.

hope

love

dream

rosemary

a love so sweet

Wedding Shower, June 1943

Wedding Shower Combine color copies of vintage fabrics with
heritage photos to evoke retro charm.

Bon Voyage A combination of vintage wallpaper and contemporary patterned papers creates a fresh twist on a distinctive heritage layout.

Childhood Memories This unique heart-shaped pocket is a charming
way to hold family documents and other treasures.

ALBERT & ZELLA were married in Kansas on August 3, 1920. Zella's father, Robert Smith, performed the wedding ceremony in the Friend's Church, where he was minister. It was not the custom of the Friends at that time to wear jewelry, so Zella and Albert did not have wedding rings. Albert gave Zella her rings about 1931.

For their honeymoon they took the train to Southern California, where Albert showed his bride the places he had discovered when he was a student at Optometry School.

They settled for six months in Salem, Oregon, and then moved to the pretty small town of McMinnville, 25 miles northwest of Salem. There, Albert set up his optometry practice.

Albert and Zella's first house was on 10th Street, which at that time was on the edge of town. After their daughter, Dorothy, was born in 1922, Albert designed and built a new home at 639 10th Street on what had been a vacant lot next door. He and Zella lived in that house for forty years. Their son Richard was born at home in 1923.

SWEET MEMORIES

Albert & Zella To preserve precious vintage postcards, work with color copies instead of original photos and memorabilia. Rub the edges gently with baby wipes or extra-fine sandpaper to create a convincing aged effect.

True Joy Create an unexpected faux vintage embellishment by aging
a die-cut metallic doily with sepia rubber-stamp ink.

chapter **5**

Elegant Visions

Designing with Translucent Materials

Add sophistication by combining
your favorite sheer materials.

WRAP ME UP IN·THY LOVE

CHRISTINA ROSETTI

Wrap Me Up The subtle layering of translucent materials, including embossed
vellums and tulle, create a sense of dimension and light.

Tokens of Affection Pages from a turn-of-the-century autograph
book are sweetly tucked into vellum heart pockets.

Divas in Laguna I A translucent curtain of patterned vellum is creatively trimmed and layered over a colorful photograph.

Divas in Laguna II Unique photo frames take shape with layered vellum secured by decorative machine-stitching.

Tickled Pink Card, True Friend Card & Prince Charming Card
Preprinted vellum expressions become the focal point
for these distinctive greeting cards.

tickled
pink

A true *friend*
is the greatest
of all blessings.

prince
charming

Valentine's Day A vellum title and coordinating background
paper bring new life to a vintage photograph.

THERE'S NO
PLACE MORE DELIGHTFUL
THAN HOME.

OUR FAMILY

HERITAGE

Our Family Soften the transition between blocks of patterned paper
with layers of translucent vellum quotes and headlines.

Barbara & Hugh Layer patterned vellums over coordinating solid pastel papers
to reduce contrast and bring attention to the central photograph.

Family Christmas A richly colored vellum headline placed over
flocked damask completes an elegant layout.

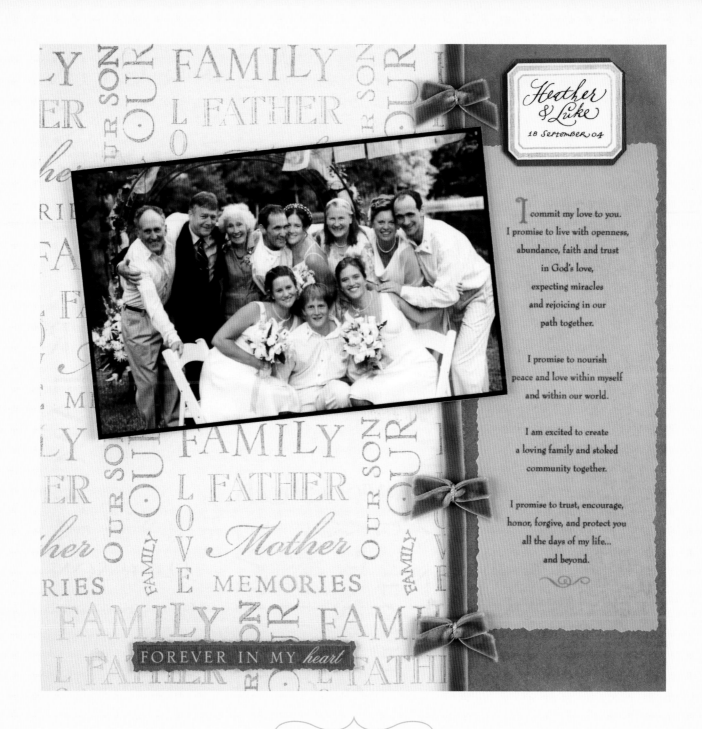

Heather & Luke
18 September 04

I commit my love to you.
I promise to live with openness,
abundance, faith and trust
in God's love,
expecting miracles
and rejoicing in our
path together.

I promise to nourish
peace and love within myself
and within our world.

I am excited to create
a loving family and stoked
community together.

I promise to trust, encourage,
honor, forgive, and protect you
all the days of my life...
and beyond.

FOREVER IN MY *heart*

Heather & Luke Romantic wedding vows are printed onto plain vellum and
layered over metallic gold paper for an elegant and sophisticated effect.

chapter **6**

First
Impressions

Adding a Personal Touch to Your Papers

*Create extraordinary
paper patterns with stamps,
stencils, and punches.*

School Days Give decorative frames instant age by applying a thin
layer of sepia rubber-stamp ink with a stencil brush.

Baby Squares Brass stencils create distinctive effects. Use a burnishing tool to produce elegant
embossed patterns, or use blending chalks to produce softly colored graphic motifs.

OUR HERITAGE

GRANDFATHER

Grandmother

Grandma and Grandpa noticed each other for the first time in 1918 at a church social, but never said a word to each other. They met again 2 years later and fell in love soon after. They married that same year and soon settled in Bismark, South Dakota, where Great Grandfather Lawson ran the family cattle ranch.

Vintage Couple Apply sepia rubber-stamp ink and pastel blending chalks with a stencil brush to beautifully distress photos and frames.

Merci Card, Birthday Wishes Card & Cherish Baby Card
Brass stencils, rubber stamps, and embossing
powder give greeting cards a touch of classic
elegance.

Birthday Wishes

merci

Olivia Create one-of-a-kind borders, frames, and
ribbons, using your favorite rubber stamps.

The Hawkins Sisters

Olivia Hawkins, my grandmother, grew up in St. Louis, Missouri. She was the oldest of five girls. Olivia loved her sisters and spent long afternoons playing outdoors with them, picking beautiful flowers in the gardens surrounding their home.

Olivia, age 7

Ruth and Peggy

Nelly and Louisa

The Hawkins Sisters Moistening blending chalks and applying them through brass stencils with a foam applicator can create softly colored graphic motifs.

Sheila Jane Card & Tulips Card
Using a common hole punch or a decorative pattern punch assures consistent and accurate cutouts every time.

Vintage Birthday Card & Bouquet Birthday Card
A thin layer of modeling paste, applied through a brass stencil, is a simple and quick method of creating a dramatic, sculptural relief. Blending chalks rubbed over an already embossed surface create a more subtle effect.

June 7, 1932

Fiona Rose Bring a beautiful, painterly feel to hand-stamped papers
by selectively applying multiple colors of ink to rubber stamps.

chapter 7

Capturing the
Moment

Unique Frames to Showcase Memories

*Surround your cherished photos
with a delightful selection of shapes
and patterns.*

Stephanie & Nick Aged edges, leather cord, and grommets combine to
give these Victorian-inspired frames a touch of vintage charm.

Paris Miniature frames playfully showcase these small-scale travel photos.

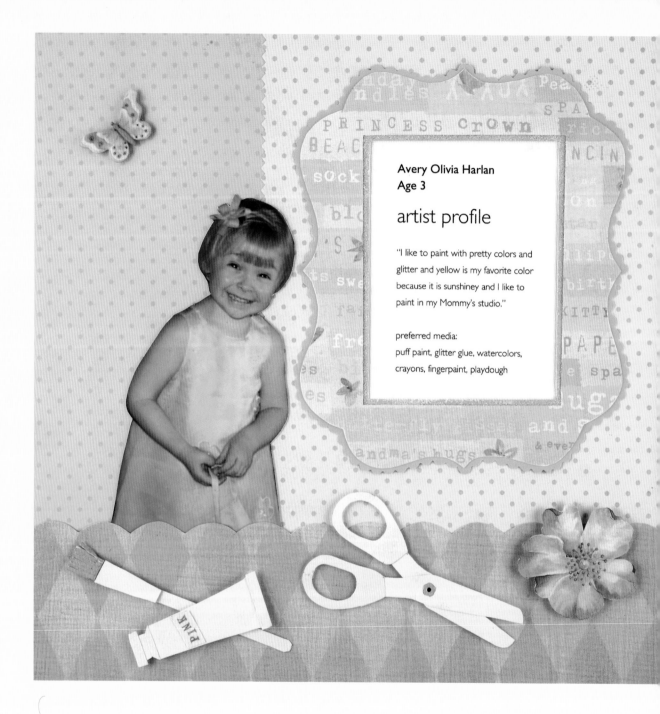

**Avery Olivia Harlan
Age 3**

artist profile

"I like to paint with pretty colors and glitter and yellow is my favorite color because it is sunshiney and I like to paint in my Mommy's studio."

preferred media:
puff paint, glitter glue, watercolors, crayons, fingerpaint, playdough

Artist Profile I The creative young artist's profile is showcased in a dimensional frame decorated with glitter and a scalloped edge.

That's You, Mommy, 2004
puff paint, crayon, watercolor on
watercolor paper

My Handprint, 2004
#1 in a series
craft paint on construction pape

The artist at work, 2004

My Handprint, 2004
#2 in a series
craft paint on construction paper

Rainbow Sky, 2004
watercolor on watercolor paper

Artist Profile II The artist's work is presented in a playful
arrangement of oversized slide frames.

{ 97 }

Betty Irena Multiple layers of patterned paper and dimensional embellishments
build a dramatic and beautiful focal point for the page.

Diorama
A traditional Victorian diorama was the inspiration
for this distinctive, multilayered wall hanging.

Heart Pocket

As cards or wall hangings, pockets are an inventive way to showcase family photos and other personal treasures.

Grandpa & Baby Jack

Combine a preprinted decorative frame with a favorite family photo and a bit of ribbon to instantly create a memorable greeting card.

Flower Girl Card

The bouquet featured in the
photograph provides inspiration
for dressing up the decorative frame
which surrounds it.

STORY

TIME

INSPIRE

Stephanie's love of reading began at the age of five, when she was a student in Mrs. Brown's class. All week long, Steph looked forward to Story Time with great enthusiasm. Her favorite story was Peter Rabbit. She and her friend Mark were mesmerized and greatly amused.

Story Time The variety of frame shapes, styles, and patterns adds to the whimsical personality of this layout.

Darling Maeve A clear dome frame brings unexpected
shine and focus to the featured photo.

Sugar

and spice

and

everything

nice

DELIGHT

Snips

and snails

and puppy

dog's

tails

Sugar & Spice Contrasting, folded edges create a page design in which
the entire layout becomes the frame for one central image.

Baby Rachel
Decorative paper is wrapped around two
layers of foam core to create a memorable and heart-felt wall hanging.

chapter 8

The Shape of Things

Innovative & Whimsical Layout Ideas

*Get inspired with these unique
and inventive layouts.*

Josephine & Kyle Add a sense of drama to whimsical layouts by creating theatrical curtains pulled back to reveal the featured photo.

Our Wedding Layers of carefully trimmed decorative paper combine to create
a large-scale pocket for treasured photos and documents.

Zella's Garden Create cutouts from large-scale photos to add a
lively and dramatic effect to collage layouts.

Paulee Angel
Collect handmade greetings and vintage paper
crafts to incorporate into future layouts.

Welcome, little one!

OUR
LITTLE
TREASURE

dream

Aaron's Birth Day I Subtle and sweetly patterned papers add
softness and warmth to black-and-white photos.

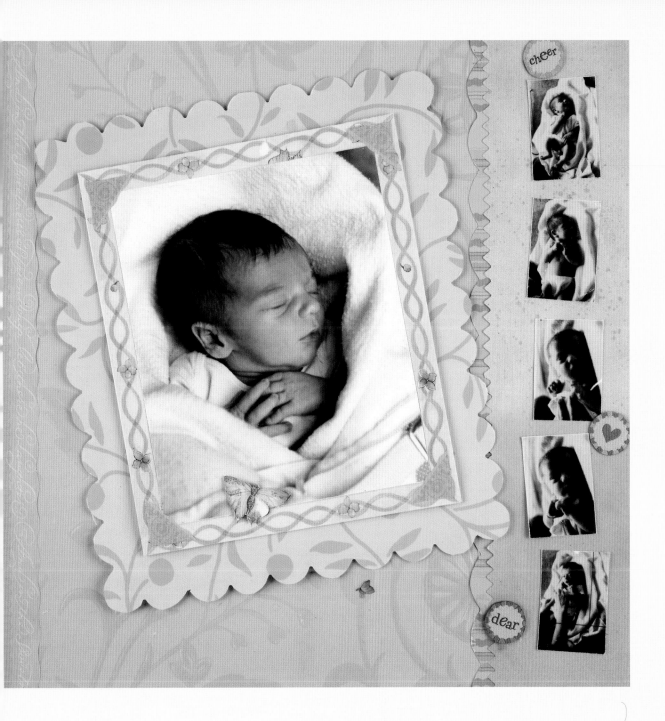

Aaron's Birth Day II A border of contact sheet photos is an effective way to display multiple images in a limited amount of space.

dorothy & hannah
bern, switzerland
july 1998

little darlings

Little Darlings A French memo-board format creates an original
and eye-catching display for framed photos.

Hugs & Kisses A delightful three-dimensional pinwheel evokes
the fun and adventure of a memorable birthday.

Templates

To use templates, simply follow these easy steps:

1. On a photocopier, enlarge or reduce selected template image to desired size. Loosely trim around edges of template.

2. Select decorative paper. If the shape is to be raised with foam dots, adhere the decorative paper to posterboard for added stiffness.

3. Apply a few dots of repositionable adhesive to back of template. Adhere template to decorative paper.

4. To facilitate detailed cutting, loosely cut around edges of template and decorative paper, leaving about ⅛" of space around the edges.

5. Use regular or decorative-edged scissors or craft knife to cut along edges of shape. Discard template. Adhere shape to project.

6. For dimension, adhere with foam dots.

7. Add glitter, sequins, beads, ribbon, stitching, or buttons for additional embellishment.

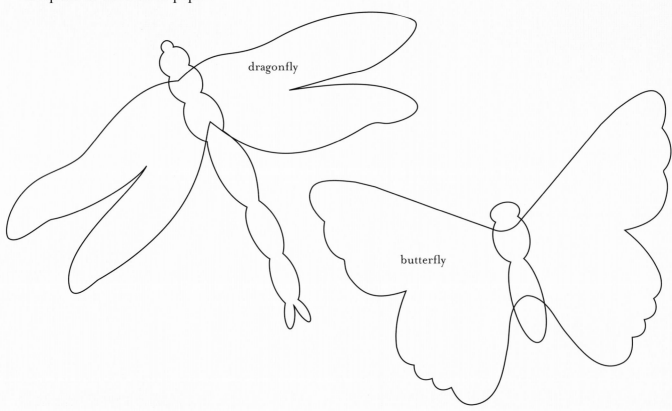

dragonfly

butterfly

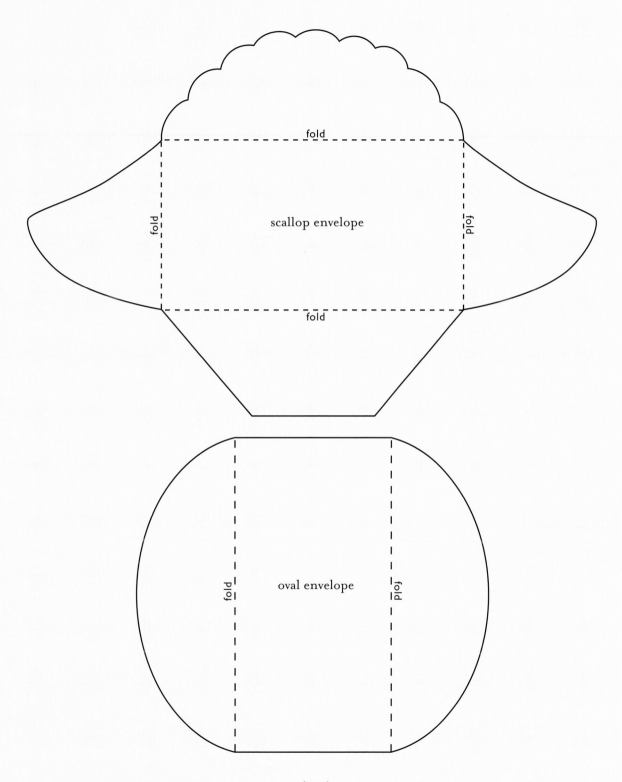

scallop envelope

fold

fold

fold

fold

oval envelope

fold

fold

heart and arrow

heart pocket

heart

fold

fold

fold

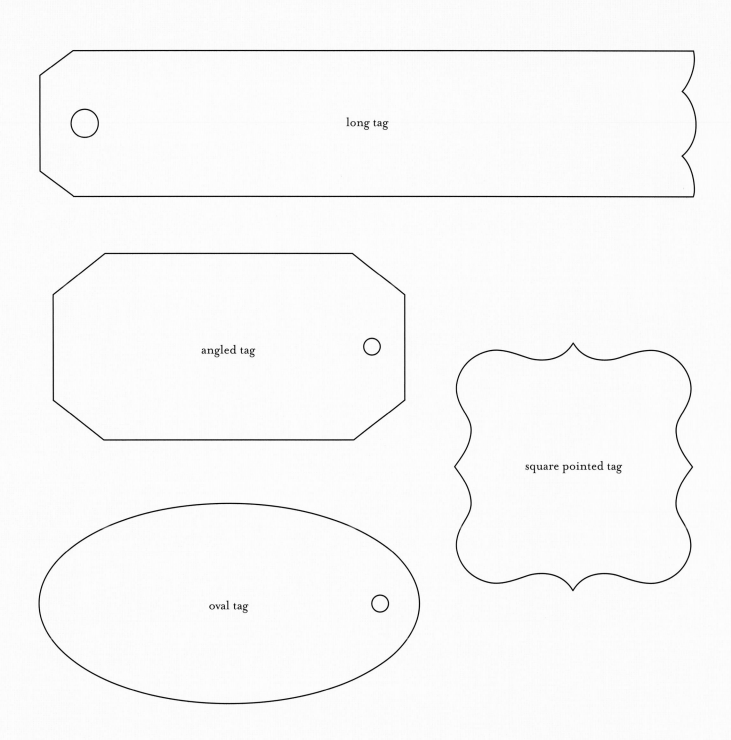

long tag

angled tag

square pointed tag

oval tag

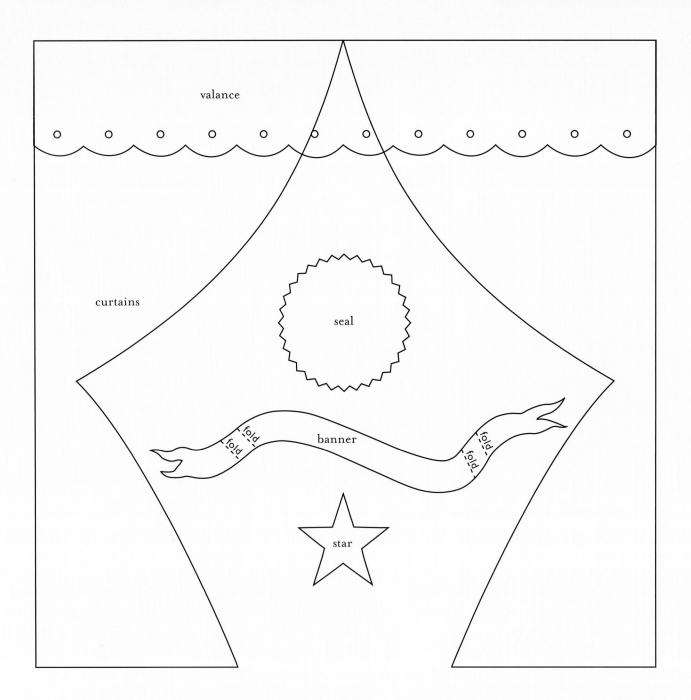

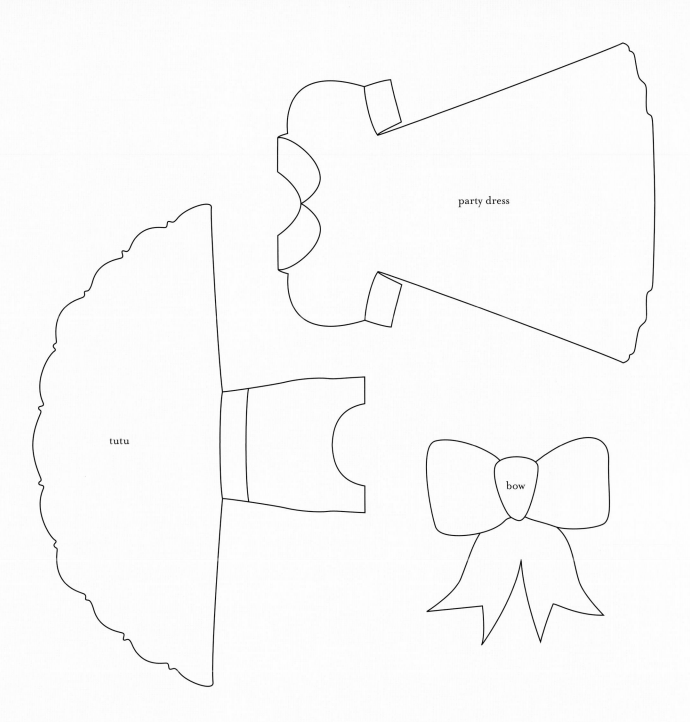

party dress

tutu

bow

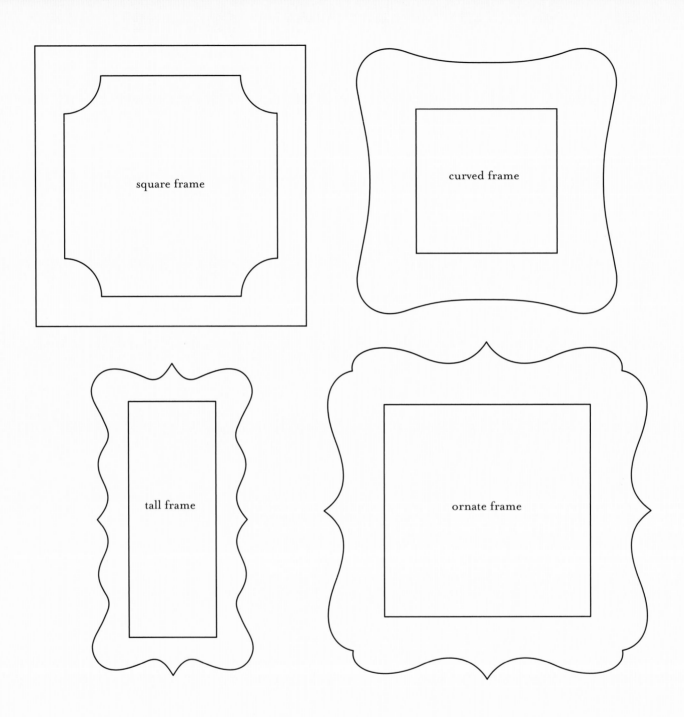

square frame

curved frame

tall frame

ornate frame

frame

wreath

Materials List

All item numbers refer to K&Company products, unless otherwise noted. Elements not identified may be found at craft and fabric stores, or at tag sales and flea markets.

Chapter 1: Mix it Up

Page 22: *Party Doll*

Design: Patricia Loftus

Papers: 1 sheet Pink Stripes (#633827), 1 sheet Romanza Wild Roses Embossed Paper (#633209), 1 sheet Romanza Wild Roses Embossed Vellum (#633216), 1 sheet Flora Bella Dots (#633193), 1 sheet Chloe Scattered Flowers (#633537), 1 sheet Mint Dot (#633858), cream card stock

Materials: Somerset Large Alphabet (#553484), ribbon, pink wedding tulle, beads, rhinestones, glitter, machine stitching, adhesive dots

Page 23: *Sisters*

Design: Valerie Salmon

Papers: 1 sheet Somerset Diamonds (#636842), 1 sheet Somerset Roses & Vines (#638754)

Materials: Emma Antiques Images Glitter (#551947), Somerset Words Metal Arts (#563124), Friend Phrases Rub-on Transfers (#590182), ribbon, buttons, fabric flower

Page 24: *Aaron at 24*

Design: Brenda Walton

Photo: Hope Harris

Papers: 1 sheet Brianna Red Damask (#637146), 1 sheet Brianna Ledger & Script (#638983), 1 sheet Brianna Large Dots (#639034), 1 sheet Brianna Birds (#639003), 1 sheet Green Stripe (#638501), 1 sheet Bella Die-cut Sheet (#651128), 1 sheet Amelia Gingham (#638822), 1 sheet green card stock, 1 sheet gold card stock, 1 sheet cream card stock

Materials: Somerset words (#563124), Plaid/All Night Media Tulip Punch (#45TLP), Plaid/All Night Media Songbird Punch (#45BBR), Plaid/All Night Media Flower Punch (#45BFL), Plaid/All Night Media Seal Punch (#45SEL), Plaid/All Night Media Pineapple Punch, Plaid/All Night Media Floral Punch (#60BFL), 1 cardboard slide mount, buttons, raffia, brass brads, natural raffia

Page 25: *Floral Birthday Card*

Design: Patricia Loftus

Papers: Chelsea Dots on Aqua (#635371), Bella Folk Art (#634541)

Materials: Floral Bella Florals Grand Adhesions (#554115)

Page 25: *Birthday Boy Tag*

Design: Brenda Walton

Papers: I sheet Aqua Small Plaid (#634121), I sheet Favorite Things for Boys (#638877), orange card stock

Materials: Celebrations Towering Type (#553583), Birthday Boy Rimmed Tags (#564459), ribbon

Pages 26: *Garden Wedding I*

Design: Sheila Herrin and Brenda Walton

Papers: I sheet Somerset Bouquet (#636156), I sheet Somerset Swirls (#636002), I sheet Somerset Stripes & Flowers (#638723), I sheet Somerset Diamonds (#636842), cream card stock, pink card stock

Materials: Somerset Words Clearly Yours (#557710), Somerset Florals & Corners Glitter Embossed Stickers (#551596), ribbon

Page 27: *Garden Wedding II*

Design: Sheila Herrin and Brenda Walton

Papers: I sheet Somerset Bouquet (#636156), I sheet Somerset Swirls (#636002), I sheet Somerset Stripes & Flowers (#638723), I sheet Somerset Diamonds (#636842), cream card stock, pink card stock

Materials: Somerset Florals & Corners Glitter Embossed Stickers (#551596), velvet leaf

Page 28: *Pink Gift Bag*

Design: Patricia Loftus

Papers: I sheet Garden Party Large Roses (#635449)

Materials: Dorset Cherry Borders (#550510), Garden Party Large Frame Grand Adhesions (#554221), ribbon, ribbon flower accent

Page 28: *Orange Gift Bag*

Design: Patricia Loftus

Papers: I sheet Chloe Vine Stripe (#633131), I sheet Orange & Pink Diamonds (#635401), cream card stock

Materials: ribbon, ribbon flower accents

Page 29: *Elinor & Sisters*

Design: Brenda Walton

Papers: I sheet Aqua Small Plaid (#634121), I sheet Aqua & Citrus Diamonds (#635234), I sheet Juliana Blocks (#633070), 2 sheets Dorset Florals Embossed (#634633), I sheet Dorset Stripes (#635258), I sheet Brianna Gingham (#639010), cream card stock

Materials: ribbon, plastic charm

Page 30: *Cousins*

Design: Patricia Loftus

Papers: I sheet Chelsea Dots on Aqua (#635371), I sheet Multicolored Diamonds (#635340),

I sheet Gingham (#633247), I sheet
Somerset Swirls (636002), I sheet
cream card stock

Materials: Dollhouse Towering
Type stickers (#533613), Inspirational Rimmed Tags (#554411),
Romanza Die-cut Alphabet
(553026), ribbon, fabric flowers

Page 31: *Happiness*

Design: Valerie Salmon

Papers: I sheet Favorite Things for
Girls (#638877), I sheet Somerset
Lavender Stripes (#738761)

Materials: Somerset Words Metal
Arts (#563124), Somerset Words
Clearly Yours (#557710), Emma
Inspirations Grand Adhesions
(#554488), Memory Phrases Rub-on
Transfers (#590175), rick rack,
ribbon, button

Chapter 2: From the Heart

Page 34: *Emma Elizabeth*

Design: Brenda Walton

Photo: Diana Kay

Papers: I sheet Pink Stripes
(#633827), I sheet Chloe Mint Dot
(#633858), I sheet Orange & Pink
Diamonds (#635401), I sheet Dorset
Large Dots (#635227), I sheet Aqua
& Olive Folk Art Floral (#635364),
I sheet cream card stock

Materials: Juliana Clearly Yours
(#557321), Chelsea Journal Tags

Clearly Yours (#557338), Tags
— clear (#557437), ribbon

Page 35: *Dreams*

Design: Brenda Walton

Papers: I sheet Favorite Things
for Boys (#638877), I sheet Dorset
Blocks (#635241), I sheet Aqua Small
Plaid Embossed (#634497)

Materials: Celebrations Towering
Type (#553583), Tags — clear
(#557437), Chloe Die-cut Alphabet
(#553002), Juliana Die-cut Alphabet
(#553019), Casual Alphabet Clearly
Yours (#280038), leather cord,
grommets

Page 36: *Paris, 1925*

Design: Patricia Loftus

Papers: I sheet Brianna Roses
(#639027), I sheet Brianna Ledger
& Script (#638983), I sheet Brianna
Damask (#637146), I sheet Bella Folk
Art (#634541), I sheet Green Stripe
(#638501)

Materials: Maison Towering Type
(#553569), Friendship Rimmed
Tags (#564435), buttons, glassine
envelope

Page 37: *Nested Boxes*

Design: Patricia Loftus

Papers: I sheet Brianna Gingham
(#639010), I sheet Brianna Red
Damask (#637146), I sheet

Brianna Large Dots (#639034),
I sheet Brianna Birds (#639003),
I sheet Brianna Text & Botanicals
(#638976)

Materials: Inspirational Rimmed
Tags (#554411), Brianna Towering
Type (#553590), ribbon, vintage
leaves and berries

Page 38: *Sweet Mother Card*

Design: Brenda Walton

Papers: I sheet Pink Stripes
(#633827), I sheet Multicolored
Diamonds (#635340)

Materials: Somerset Florals &
Corners Glitter (#551596), Brianna
Letters & Die-cuts (#553361),
ribbon

Page 38: *Vintage Tea Party Card*

Design: Patricia Loftus

Papers: I sheet Emma Floral
Pattern (#638846), I sheet Peach
Dots (#634107)

Materials: Emma Inspirations
Grand Adhesions (#555488), vintage
floral accent

Page 39: *All Girl*

Design: Valerie Salmon

Papers: I sheet Garden Party Multi
Stripes (#635470), I sheet Dorset
Large Dots (#635227), I sheet Favorite Things For Girls (#638884), I
sheet Citrus on Pink Dots (#635487)

Materials: Fun Phrases Rub-on
Transfers (#590090), Fun Letters
Rub-on Transfers (3590106),
ribbons, rick rack, buttons, string,
flower accent

Page 40: *Love You Darling I*

Design: Brenda Walton

Papers: I sheet Brianna Block
Collage (#638990), I sheet Brianna
Gingham (#639010), I sheet Brianna
Birds (#639003), I sheet Brianna
Ledger & Script (#638983)

Materials: Brianna Letters &
Die-cut (#553361), Brianna Postage
Stamps Embossed Stickers (#551916),
Amelia Charmers (#559547),
Brianna 2 Charmers (#559585),
Brianna Images (#551602), Tags
—clear (#557437), string, glassine
envelope, flower accent, vintage
telegram, grommets

Page 41: *Love You Darling II*

Design: Brenda Walton

Papers: I sheet Brianna block
Collage (#638990), I sheet Brianna
Roses (#639027), I sheet Brianna
Birds (#639003), I sheet Brianna
Ledger &Script (#638983)

Materials: Brianna Images
Embossed Stickers (#551602), Flora
Bella Florals Grand Adhesions
(#554115), glassine envelope,
upholstery tack, rick rack, vintage
telegram, string

Page 42: *Together*

Design: Valerie Salmon

Papers: 1 sheet Aqua Painted Diamonds (#635463), 1 sheet Aqua Small Plaid (#634121), 1 sheet Berry Floral (#634213)

Materials: Family Phrases Rub-on Transfers (#590083), ribbon, button, ink

Page 43: *Forever*

Design: Brenda Walton

Photos: Beth Baugher

Papers: 1 sheet Ivory Chelsea Blind Embossed (#635326), 1 sheet Citrus on Pink Dots (#635487)

Materials: Neopolitan Towering Type (#553538), ribbon

Page 44: *Forever in My Heart*

Design: Brenda Walton

Papers: 1 sheet Somerset Roses & Vines (#638754), 1 sheet Somerset Small Floral (#638730), 1 sheet Somerset Diamonds (#636842), 1 sheet Somerset Stripes & Flowers (#638723), 1 sheet Somerset Swirls (#636002), 1 sheet cream card stock

Materials: Somerset Die-cut Alphabet (#553293), Somerset Oval Frame (#555402), Somerset Florals & Corners Glitter Embossed Stickers (#551596), ribbon, sequins

Page 45: *Kate Box*

Design: Patricia Loftus

Papers: 1 sheet Somerset Stripes & Flowers (#638723), 1 sheet Somerset Swirls (#636002), 1 sheet Garden Party Large Dots (#635456)

Materials: Dollhouse Towering Type (#553613), Chloe Borders Embossed Stickers (#552449)

Chapter 3: On the Surface

Page 48: *Sweet Friend*

Design: Valerie Salmon

Papers: 1 sheet Somerset Diamonds (#636842), 1 sheet Somerset Lavender Stripes (#638761), 1 sheet Juliana Die-cut Sheet (#651067)

Materials: Emma Inspirations Grand Adhesions (#555488), Friend Phrases Rub-on Transfers (#590182), ribbon, fabric flowers

Page 49: *Gift Tags*

Design: Patricia Loftus, Charlotte Lyons and Brenda Walton

Papers: 1 sheet Emma Floral Pattern (#638846), 1 sheet Orange & Pink Diamonds (#635401), 1 sheet Emma Blocks (#638907)

Materials: Somerset Friendship Tags (#555419), Brianna Postage Stamps (#551916), Emma Inspirations Grand Adhesions (#555488), ribbon

Page 50: *Vintage Classroom*

Design: Brenda Walton

Papers: I sheet Bella French Wallpaper (#635944), I sheet Bella Acorn Embossed (#634510), I sheet Bella Gems (#634558), cream card stock, metallic green card stock gold card stock

Materials: Bella Die-cut Alphabet (#553064), Brianna Images (#551602), ribbon, wax seal

Page 51: *Hope & Devotion*

Design: Valerie Salmon

Papers: I sheet Bella Bordered (#635296), I sheet Plum & Olive Diamonds (#634572), I sheet Bella Acorn (#634534), cream card stock

Materials: Brianna Florals Embossed Stickers (#551633), Words & Expressions Rub-on Transfers (#590076), buttons, ribbons

Page 52: *Sierra*

Design: Valerie Salmon

Papers: I sheet Peach Dots (#634107), I sheet Gingham (#633247), I sheet Somerset Bouquet (#636156)

Materials: Friend Phrases Rub-on Transfers (#590182), Somerset Friendship Tags Grand Adhesions (#555419), Emma Inspirations Grand Adhesions (#555488), Somerset Die-cut Alphabet (#553293), ribbon, photo corners

Page 53: *Somerset*

Design: Brenda Walton

Papers: I Somerset Scrap Kit (#670082), pale green card stock, pale pink card stock

Materials: 12" x 12" Ivory Scallop wood frame (#390171), ribbon

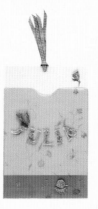

Page 54: *Julia Card*

Design: Patricia Loftus

Papers: I sheet Garden Party Aqua Floral Printed Embossed Vellum (#634619), cream card stock

Materials: Somerset Florals & Corners Glitter Embossed Stickers (#551596), Romanza Dimensional Alphabet

Page 54: *Amy Card*

Design: Brenda Walton

Papers: I sheet Chloe Awning Stripe (#633582), I sheet olive green card stock, I sheet periwinkle card stock

Materials: Shelby Towering Type (#553576), Formal Alphabet Clearly Yours (#280021), I Plaid/All Night Media Dianthus Vine Brass Stencil (#5670S), grommets, paper flower

Page 55: *Dress Card*

Design: Patricia Loftus

Papers: 1 sheet Orange & Pink Diamonds (#635401)

Materials: 2 sheets Brenda's Bows Grand Adhesions (#554245), Wild Roses Banners & Borders Embossed Stickers (#552555)

Page 55: *Niece Card*

Design: Brenda Walton

Papers: 1 sheet Chelsea Pink (#635302), 1 sheet Pink Stripes (#633827)

Materials: Family Phrases Rub-on Transfers (#590083), pink card stock, cream card stock, button

Page 56: *Party Favor Bag*

Design: Patricia Loftus

Papers: 1 sheet Garden Party Aqua Floral (#634596), 1 sheet Citrus on Pink Dots (#635487)

Materials: Romanza Collage Flowers Grand Adhesions (#554054), ribbon

Page 57: *By the Sea*

Design: Brenda Walton

Papers: 1 sheet Mint Dot (#633858), 1 sheet Romanza Awning Stripe (#633230), 1 sheet Floral & Bird Damask (#633575), cream card stock

Materials: Chloe Die-cut Alphabet (#553002), Chloe By The Sea Grand Adhesions (#554108)

Page 58: *Purse Gift Tags*

Design: Melissa Neufeld

Papers: 1 sheet Somerset Engraving (#638747), Brenda's Card Pad (#259010), cream card stock

Materials: Brenda's Photo Corners Clearly Yours (#557277), Juliana Clearly Yours (#557321), Chelsea Words Clearly Yours (#557260), Chelsea Borders Clearly Yours (#557369), silk damask fabric, velvet ribbon, grosgrain ribbon

Page 59: *Believe*

Design: Valerie Salmon

Papers: 1 sheet Favorite Things for Girls (#638884), 1 sheet Emma Blocks (#638907), 1 sheet Somerset Swirls (#636002)

Materials: Somerset Words Metal Arts (#563124), Memory Phrases Rub-on Transfers (#590175), Friend Phrases Rub-on Transfers (#590182), Somerset Florals & Corners Glitter Stickers (#551586), Emma Inspirations Grand Adhesions (#555488), ribbon, rick rack

Chapter 4: Vintage Charm

Page 62: *Tea Party*

Design: Brenda Walton

Papers: 1 sheet Plum & Olive Diamonds (#634572), 1 sheet Bella Folk Art (#634541), 1 sheet Brianna Birds (#639003), 1 sheet Brianna Large Dots (#639034), 1 sheet Green Stripe (#638501), 1 sheet Amelia Gingham (#638822), cream card stock

Materials: Maison Towering Type (#553569), Bella Borders (#557383), button, string, small brass hinges, ribbon, rick rack, brass brads, fabric flower

Page 63: *Sewing Box*

Design: Sheila Herrin

Papers: 1 sheet Amelia Diamonds & Stripes (#638778), 1 sheet Amelia Gingham (#638822), 1 sheet Amelia Large Flowers (#637023)

Materials: Amelia Borders Embossed Stickers (#551497), Brass Scissors (#558465), bobbin, rhinestone, measuring tape

Page 64: *Sweet Baby*

Design: Valerie Salmon

Papers: 1 sheet Multicolored Diamonds (#635340), 1 sheet Bella Acorn embossed (#634510), pink card stock

Materials: Family Phrases Rub-on Transfers (#590083), Borders & Frames Rub-on Transfers (#590069), ribbons, buttons

Page 65: *Wedding Shower*

Design: Brenda Walton

Photo: Stephanie Loftus

Papers: 1 sheet Gingham (#633247), 1 sheet Orange & Pink Diamonds (#635401), 1 sheet Chloe Painted Dots (#633568), 1 sheet Citrus Dots (#633261)

Materials: Somerset Florals & Corners (#551596), Casual Alphabet Clearly Yours (#280038), Brenda's Card Pad #2 (#259010), Chelsea Fruit & Flower Images (#554153), rick rack

Page 66: *Bon Voyage*

Design: Patricia Loftus and Brenda Walton

Papers: 1 sheet Chelsea Dots on Aqua (#635371), 1 sheet Bella Bordered (#635296), 1 sheet Somerset Swirls (#636002), 1 sheet Amelia Vine Flowers (#638785), gold card stock, cream card stock

Materials: Emma Large Alphabet (#553477), vintage postcard, wallpapers, letter, button, metal embellishment, ribbon

Page 67: *Childhood Memories*

Design: Patricia Loftus and Brenda Walton

Papers: 1 sheet Amelia Large Flowers Embossed Vellum (#637047), 1 sheet Amelia Diamonds & Stripes (#638778), 1 sheet Brianna Large Dots (#639034), 1 sheet Brianna Gingham (#639010), 1 sheet Brianna Ledger & Script, 1 sheet Amelia Painted Dots (#638808)

Materials: Brianna Words Metal Arts (#563131), vintage watch faces, vintage letter & envelopes, ribbons, glassine envelope, fabric leaf, brass grommets

Page 68: *Albert & Zella*

Design: Patricia Loftus

Papers: 1 sheet Somerset Engraving (#638747), cream card stock

Materials: Amelia Journal Tags Foil (#551909), Somerset Large Alphabet (#553484), 2 sheets Somerset Images (#554894), Somerset Journal Tags Foil (#551626), vintage hat pin, postcard, ribbon

Page 69: *True Joy*

Design: Patricia Loftus

Papers: 1 sheet Somerset Bouquet Embossed (#636132), pink card stock, periwinkle blue paper, cream card stock

Materials: Somerset Florals & Corners Glitter Embossed Stickers

(#551596), Words & Expressions Rub-on Transfers (#590076), Borders & Frames Rub-on Transfers (#560069), Tags —clear (#557437), glassine envelope, ribbon, vintage doily, vintage sheet music

Chapter 5: Elegant Visions

Page 72: *Wrap Me Up*

Design: Brenda Walton

Papers: 2 sheets Juliana Blocks (#633070), 1 sheet Juliana Lilacs Embossed Vellum (#633056), 1 sheet Pearlessence Swirl Blind Embossed Vellum (#633841), 1 Juliana Die-cut Sheet (# 651067), silver card stock

Materials: Juliana Clearly Yours (#557321), ribbons

Page 73: *Tokens of Affection*

Design: Brenda Walton

Papers: 1 sheet Romanza Wild Roses Embossed Vellum (#633216), 1 sheet Garden Party Pink Floral Embossed Velum (#634664), 1 sheet Chelsea Pink Embossed Vellum (#634442), 1 sheet Garden Party Pink Floral (#634602), 1 sheet Peach Dots (#634107), 1 sheet Pink Stripes (#633827), 1 sheet Chelsea Pink (#635302), cream card stock

Materials: Garden Party Tags (#559240), vintage postage stamp, vintage correspondence

Page 74: *Divas in Laguna I*

Design: Brenda Walton

Photo: Todd Clark

Papers: 1 sheet Emma Blocks (#638907), 1 sheet Antiques Floral Vines Embossed Vellum (#637542), 1 sheet Emma Diamonds (#638860)

Materials: Chloe by the Sea Grand Adhesion (#554108), fringe, sequins, glassine envelope

Page 75: *Divas in Laguna II*

Design: Brenda Walton

Papers: 1 sheet Emma Blocks (#638907), 1 sheet Antiques Floral Vines Embossed Vellum (#637542)

Materials: Chloe by the Sea Grand Adhesion (#554108), fringe, sequins, rhinestone stars

Page 76: *Tickled Pink Card*

Design: Brenda Walton

Papers: 1 sheet Pink Romanza Blind Embossed (#633322), pink card stock

Materials: Quotable Notables Expressions & Sayings (#626041), ribbon

Page 76: *True Friend Card*

Design: Patricia Loftus

Papers: 1 sheet Small Chelsea Vine Flowers Glitter (#635333)

Materials: Quotable Notables Love & Friendship (#626058), Romanza Journal Tags (#552470), Romanza Images (552494)

Page 76: *Prince Charming Card*

Design: Brenda Walton

Papers: pale aqua card stock

Materials: Quotable Notables Expressions & Sayings (#626041), ribbon

Page 77: *Valentine's Day*

Design: Patricia Loftus

Papers: 1 sheet Garden Party Large Roses (#635449), 1 sheet Citrus on Pink Dots (#635487), gold card stock

Materials: Quotable Notables (#626034), gold ink, ribbon

Page 78: *Our Family*

Design: Brenda Walton

Photo: Ed Peckham

Papers: 1 sheet Mint Dot (#633858), 1 sheet Chelsea Dots on Aqua (#635371)

Materials: Somerset Florals & Corners Glitter Embossed Stickers (#551596), Quotable Notables Family (#626027), Brenda's Card Pad #2 (#259010), Chelsea Blue Borders Clearly Yours (#557369), ribbon

Page 79: *Barbara & Hugh*

Design: Brenda Walton

Papers: I sheet Dorset Flowers Embossed Vellum (#634640), I sheet Aqua Small Plaid (#634121), I sheet Aqua Gems (#634114)

Materials: Dorset Journal Tags (#552999), Dorset Botanical (#552920), Dorset Dimensional Borders (#554696)

Page 80: *Family Christmas*

Design: Brenda Walton

Papers: I sheet Brianna Green Damask Flocked (#637139), I sheet Brianna Gingham (#639010), I sheet Pearlessence Swirl Blind Embossed Vellum (#633841), gold card stock, platinum card stock, cream card stock, green card stock

Materials: Quotable Notables Holiday & Vacation (#626034), ribbon, brass grommets, string, vintage embellishments, glassine envelope

Page 81: *Heather & Luke*

Design: Brenda Walton

Photo: Beth Baugher

Papers: I sheet cream card stock, I sheet solid green metallic paper

Materials: velvet ribbon, rubber stamps, gold ink

Chapter 6: First Impressions

Page 84: *School Days*

Design: Patricia Loftus

Papers: I sheet Brianna Gingham (#639010), I sheet Brianna Block Collage (#638990), I sheet Brianna Large Dots (#639034), I sheet Brianna Brianna Roses (#639027), I sheet Brianna Text & Botanicals

Materials: Brianna Images Embossed Stickers (#551602), grommets, sepia ink, glassine envelope, button, ribbon, vintage watch face, wooden paper clip

Page 85: *Baby Squares*

Design: Brenda Walton

Papers: cream card stock, pink card stock, gold card stock, coral card stock

Materials: All Night Media/Plaid Brass Stencil (#5670S), ribbon, grommets

Page 86: *Vintage Couple*

Design: Patricia Loftus

Papers: I sheet Somerset Diamonds (#636842), I sheet Somerset Bouquet Embossed (#636132), pink card stock, cream card stock

Materials: ribbon, wooden paper clip, sepia ink

Page 87: *Merci Card*

Design: Brenda Walton

Papers: 1 sheet Emma Diamonds (#636842), 1 sheet Garden Party Large Roses (#635449), cream card stock, gold card stock, vellum

Materials: ribbon, vintage sheet music, rubber stamps

Page 87: *Birthday Wishes Card*

Design: Patricia Loftus

Papers: cream card stock, pink card stock

Materials: ribbon, green ink, rubber stamps

Page 87: *Cherish Baby Card*

Design: Brenda Walton

Papers: pink card stock, cream card stock

Materials: rubber stamps, ribbon, gold ink

Page 88: *Olivia*

Design: Sheila Herrin

Papers: 1 sheet aqua card stock, 1 sheet periwinkle blue paper, 1 sheet pale green card stock

Materials: rubber stamps, buttons, magenta ink, silver ink, clear ink, gold ink, vintage floral embellishment, ribbon

Page 89: *The Hawkins Sisters*

Design: Patricia Loftus

Papers: 1 sheet Garden Party Multi-Stripes (#635470), 1 sheet Flora Bella Dots (#633193), 1 sheet Pink Romanza Blind Embossed (#633322), pale pink card stock, dark pink card stock, cream card stock

Materials: Plaid/All Night Media Brass Stencil (#5670S), Brianna Words Metal Arts (#563131), Dorset Floral Images Grand Adhesions (#554160), ribbon, floral embellishment, buttons, pink ink, plum ink

Page 90: *Sheila Jane Card*

Design: Brenda Walton

Papers: coral card stock, gold card stock, cream card stock

Materials: Plaid/All Night Media Brass Stencil (#5670S), blending chalks, ribbon, rubber stamp

Page 90: *Tulips Card*

Design: Patricia Loftus and Anna Pasquale

Papers: 1 sheet Orange & Pink Diamonds (#635401), 1 sheet Flora Bella Filagree (#633179), 1 sheet Chelsea Pink (#635302), 1 sheet Emma Floral Pattern (#638846), 1 sheet Pink Stripes (#633827), green card stock

Materials: rick rack, ribbon

Page 90: *Vintage Birthday Card*

Design: Patricia Loftus

Papers: green card stock

Materials: Plaid/All Night Media Brass Stencil (#5670S), blending chalks, ribbon

Page 90: *Bouquet Birthday Card*

Design: Patricia Loftus and Anna Pasquale

Papers: 1 sheet Chelsea Pink (#635302), coral card stock, cream card stock

Materials: Plaid/All Night Media Dianthus Vase Brass Stencil (#5739S), ribbon, modeling paste

Page 91: *Fiona Rose*

Design: Brenda Walton

Papers: cream card stock, blue paper

Materials: ribbon, rubber stamps, blue ink, red ink, green ink, yellow ink, white ink

Chapter 7: Capturing the Moment

Page 94: *Stephanie & Nick*

Design: Patricia Loftus

Papers: 1 sheet Brianna Large Dots (#639034), 1 sheet Brianna Roses (#639027), 1 sheet Brianna Birds (#639003), 1 sheet Brianna Gingham (#639010), 1 sheet Brianna Ledger & Script (#638983), cream card stock, dark green metallic card stock

Materials: Brianna Florals Embossed Stickers (#551633), sepia ink, string, leather cording, button, grommets

Page 95: *Paris*

Design: Brenda Walton

Photo: Aaron Peckham

Papers: 1 sheet Garden Party Aqua Floral (#634596), 1 sheet Chelsea Dots on Aqua (#635371), 1 sheet Bella Folk Art (#634541), 1 sheet Pink Stripes (#633827), 1 sheet Orange & Pink Diamonds (#635401), pale green card stock

Materials: Chelsea Frames & Tags Grand Adhesions (#554139), Romanza Dimensional Alphabet Grand Adhesions (#554061), ribbon, vintage watch face, grommets

Page 96: *Artist Profile I*

Design: Karen Harlan

Papers: 1 sheet Emma Diamonds (#638860), 1 sheet Favorite Things For Girls (#638884), cream card stock, pink card stock

Materials: Somerset Florals & Corners Glitter Embossed Stickers (#551596), Chelsea Charmers (#559189)

Page 97: *Artist Profile II*

Design: Karen Harlan

Papers: 1 sheet Emma Diamonds (#638860), 1 sheet Favorite Things For Girls (#638884), cream card stock, pink card stock

Materials: Somerset Florals & Corners Glitter Embossed Stickers (#551596), Chelsea Charmers (#559189)

Page 98: *Betty Irena*

Design: Brenda Walton

Papers: 1 sheet Somerset Diamonds (#636842), 1 sheet Somerset Engraving (#638747), 1 sheet Pink Stripes (#633827), 1 sheet Aqua Small Plaid (#634121), 1 sheet Garden Party Pink Floral (#634602), 1 sheet Garden Party Pink Floral Vellum (#634664), cream card stock

Materials: Dorset Floral Images Grand Adhesions (#554160), Brenda's Photo Corners II Embossed Stickers (#551503), Flora Bella

Journal Tags Grand Adhesions (#554122)

Page 99: *Diorama*

Design: Patricia Loftus

Papers: 1 sheet Aqua & Citrus Diamonds (#635234), 1 sheet Chloe Awning Stripes (#633582), cream card stock

Materials: Romanza Dimensional Alphabet Grand Adhesions (#554061), Flora Bella Florals Grand Adhesions (#554115), Borders & Frames Rub-on Transfers (#590069), Juliana Borders Embossed Stickers (#552517), vintage trim, ribbon, beads

Page 100: *Heart Pocket*

Design: Brenda Walton

Papers: 1 sheet Brianna Gingham (#639010), 1 sheet Ivory Romanza Embossed (#633513), 1 sheet Flora Bella Green Pearlessence Embossed (#63339), gold paper

Materials: Plaid/All Night Media Dogwood Punch (#45DGW), vintage leaves, ribbon, vintage postcard

Page 100: *Grandpa & Baby Jack*

Design: Patricia Loftus

Papers: 1 sheet Antiqued Floral Vines (#F637528), 1 sheet Peach Dots (#634107)

Materials: ribbon

Page 101: *Flower Girl Card*

Design: Patricia Loftus

Materials: Brenda's Card Pad #2 (#259010), Somerset Florals & Corners Glitter Embossed Stickers (#551596), ribbon

Page 102: *Story Time*

Design: Patricia Loftus

Papers: 1 sheet Chloe Painted Dots (#633568), 1 sheet Lavender Damask (#634169), 1 sheet Juliana Blocks (# 633070), 1 sheet Somerset Diamonds (#636842), blue card stock, cream card stock, purple card stock

Materials: Somerset Large Alphabet (#553484), Somerset Images Grand Adhesions (#554984)

Page 103: *Darling Maeve*

Design: Brenda Walton

Photo: Beth Baugher

Papers: 1 sheet Garden Party Pink Floral Embossed Vellum (#634664), 1 sheet Peach Dots (#634107), cream card stock

Materials: Chelsea Frame Clearly Yours (#557352), ribbon, vintage flower accent

Page 104: *Sugar & Spice*

Design: Brenda Walton

Papers: 1 sheet Chloe Citrus Vines & Dots (#633544), 1 sheet Aqua Small Plaid (#634121), 1 sheet Aqua & Citrus Diamonds (#635234), 1 sheet Garden Party Pink Floral (#634602), 1 sheet Mint Dot (#633858), 1 sheet Flora Bella Dots (#633193), vellum

Materials: Chelsea Words Clearly Yours (#557260), ribbon, grommets

Page 105: *Baby Rachel*

Design: Brenda Walton

Papers: 1 sheet Favorite Things for Girls (#638884), 1 sheet Pink Stripes (#633827)

Materials: Emma Inspirations Grand Adhesions (#555488), Somerset Large Alphabet Jumbo Glitter Stickers (#553484)

Chapter 8: The Shape of Things

Page 108: *Josephine & Kyle*

Design: Karen Harlan

Papers: 1 sheet Plum & Olive Diamonds (#635296), 1 sheet Bella Folk Art (#634541), 1 sheet Bella Gems (#634558), 1 sheet Bella Acorn (#634534), 1 sheet Bella French Wallpaper (#635944), 1 sheet Bella Bordered (#635296), cream card stock, gold card stock, silver card stock

Materials: star embellishments

Page 109: *Our Wedding*

Design: Brenda Walton

Papers: 1 sheet Somerset Bouquet Embossed (#636132), 1 sheet Somerset Diamonds (#636842), 1 sheet Somerset Small Floral (#638730)

Materials: ribbons, vintage correspondence, rubber stamps, gold ink, grommets, glitter, floral embellishments

Page 110: *Zella's Garden*

Design: Brenda Walton

Papers: 1 sheet Pink Stripes (#633827), 1 sheet Emma Large Flowers (#638891), 1 sheet Orange & Pink Diamonds (#635401)

Materials: Somerset Words Clearly Yours (#557710), Emma Inspirations Grand Adhesions (#555488), rick rack, ribbon, floral embellishment, vintage correspondence

Page 111: *Paulee Angel*

Design: Brenda Walton

Papers: Brianna Ledger & Script (#638983), black paper, cream card stock

Materials: Plaid/All Night Media Dove Punch (#45FBR), ribbon, floral embellishments

Page 112: *Aaron's Birth Day I*

Design: Brenda Walton

Photos: Todd Walton

Papers: 1 sheet Embossed Suede (#633834), 1 sheet Citrus Vines & Dots (#633544), 1 sheet Juliana Die-cut Sheet (#651067), 1 sheet Chloe Awning Stripes (#633582), 1 sheet Juliana Blocks (#633070)

Materials: Chloe Die-cut Alphabet (#553002)

Page 113: *Aaron's Birth Day II*

Design: Brenda Walton

Photos: Todd Walton

Papers: 1 sheet Light Lavender Swirl Embossed (#633315), 1 sheet Embossed Suede (#633834), 1 sheet Citrus Vines & Dots (#633544), 1 sheet Juliana Die-cut Sheet (#651067), 1 sheet Chloe Awning Stripes (#633582), 1 sheet Juliana Blocks (#633070)

Materials: Juliana Dragonfly & Flowers Grand Adhesions (#554016), ribbon, bow

Page 114: *Little Darlings*

Design: Brenda Walton

Photo: Robert Peckham

Papers: 1 sheet Somerset Engraving (#638747), 1 sheet Somerset Diamonds (#636842), 1 sheet Somerset Stripes & Flowers (#638723), pink card stock, green card stock, cream card stock

Materials: Somerset Borders & Corners Glitter (#551619), Somerset Images Grand Adhesions (#554894), Somerset Words Clearly Yours (#557710), buttons

Page 115: *Hugs & Kisses*

Design: Patricia Loftus

Papers: 1 sheet Favorite Things for Girls (#638884), 1 sheet Chloe Painted Dots (#633568), 1 sheet Somerset Swirls (#636002)

Materials: Emma Inspirations Grand Adhesions (#555488)

Metric Equivalency Chart

mm-millimeters   cm-centimeters
inches to millimeters and centimeters

inches	mm	cm	inches	cm	inches	cm
1/8	3	0.3	9	22.9	30	76.2
1/4	6	0.6	10	25.4	31	78.7
1/2	13	1.3	12	30.5	33	83.8
5/8	16	1.6	13	33.0	34	86.4
3/4	19	1.9	14	35.6	35	88.9
7/8	22	2.2	15	38.1	36	91.4
1	25	2.5	16	40.6	37	94.0
1 1/4	32	3.2	17	43.2	38	96.5
1 1/2	38	3.8	18	45.7	39	99.1
1 3/4	44	4.4	19	48.3	40	101.6
2	51	5.1	20	50.8	41	104.1
2 1/2	64	6.4	21	53.3	42	106.7
3	76	7.6	22	55.9	43	109.2
3 1/2	89	8.9	23	58.4	44	111.8
4	102	10.2	24	61.0	45	114.3
4 1/2	114	11.4	25	63.5	46	116.8
5	127	12.7	26	66.0	47	119.4
6	152	15.2	27	68.6	48	121.9
7	178	17.8	28	71.1	49	124.5
8	203	20.3	29	73.7	50	127.0

Merci

I am very grateful for the many hands that helped bring this book to life. Thank you to my husband, Doug Peckham, for his patience, wisdom, and support; to my son, Aaron Miller Peckham, for his valuable technical assistance; to Anna Pasquale for her editorial expertise and creative contributions; to my friend and agent, Sheila Herrin, for her conceptual advice and guidance; to Kay Stanley, owner of K&Company, for her inspiration and support; to Efrat Rafaeli for her beautiful book design and photo styling; to Leslie Farmer for her production work; to Laurie Frankel for her gorgeous photography; to Paulee Gomke for the use of her props; to my very talented team of papercrafters, including Patricia Loftus, Sheila Herrin, Anna Pasquale, Karen Harlan, Valerie Salmon, Charlotte Lyons, Melissa Nuefeld, and Stephanie Loftus; to my editors, Jo Packham and Cindy Stoeckl, for providing me with the opportunity to write this book; to my dear friends and family, who have given me many happy memories with which to fill my scrapbooks; and to the supportive and loyal crafters who make it possible for me to continue doing what I love.

Index